Know It All!
Beginner Guides to the Big World

I0794760

Let's Learn All About
Saving Our Planet!

WINDMILL BOOKS

Published in 2025 by Windmill Books,
an Imprint of Rosen Publishing
2544 Clinton St.
Buffalo, NY 14224

Publishing Director Belinda Gallagher
Creative Director Jo Cowan
Editorial Director Rosie Neave
Senior Editor Fran Bromage
Senior Designer Emily Stalley
Image Manager Liberty Newton
Production Elizabeth Collins
Reprographics Stephan Davis
Consultant Barbara Taylor

Cataloging-in-Publication Data

Names: De la Bédoyère, Camilla, author. | Wood, Steve, illustrator.
Title: Let's learn all about saving our planet! / by Camilla de la Bédoyère, illustrated by Steve Wood.
Description: Buffalo, New York : Windmill Books, 2025. | Series: Know it all!: beginner guides to the big world
Identifiers: ISBN 9781538396018 (pbk.) | ISBN 9781538396025 (library bound) | ISBN 9781538396032 (ebook)
Subjects: LCSH: Environmental protection--Juvenile literature. | Environmentalism--Juvenile literature.
Classification: LCC TD170.15 D373 2025 | DDC 363.7--dc23

Printed in the United States of America
CPSIA Compliance Information: Batch #CSWM25: For Further Information contact Rosen Publishing at 1-800-237-9932

Find us on

Know It All!

Beginner Guides to the Big World

Let's Learn All About Saving Our Planet!

Camilla de la Bédoyère

Illustrated by Steve Wood

WINDMILL BOOKS

Contents

I'm working out the food miles of the snack I'm about to eat!

Helping our planet can be as simple as planting more flowers.

Choices you make every day, like how you travel, can make a big difference.

Our perfect planet

Earth is home to billions of living things... but it's in trouble. Let's find out more about it, and how to start looking after our planet!

Super Sun

The Earth is a rocky planet spinning through space. It travels around the Sun – a huge ball of burning gas that gives us sunlight and keeps us warm.

I CAN... SEE WHY EARTH IS PERFECT FOR LIFE

Count how many animals and plants you can see in one day. Look out of the window or go on a walk with a grown-up.

If the Sun were hollow, it would take about one million Earths to fill it!

A living planet

There are millions of different types of **living things** on Earth – all sorts of animals, plants, fungi, and really tiny things, such as bacteria.

Greenhouse Earth

The Earth's atmosphere acts like a cozy blanket around the world. It lets in sunshine, traps heat, and keeps our planet at the right temperature for life.

There is less methane than carbon dioxide in the atmosphere, but methane traps heat a lot more.

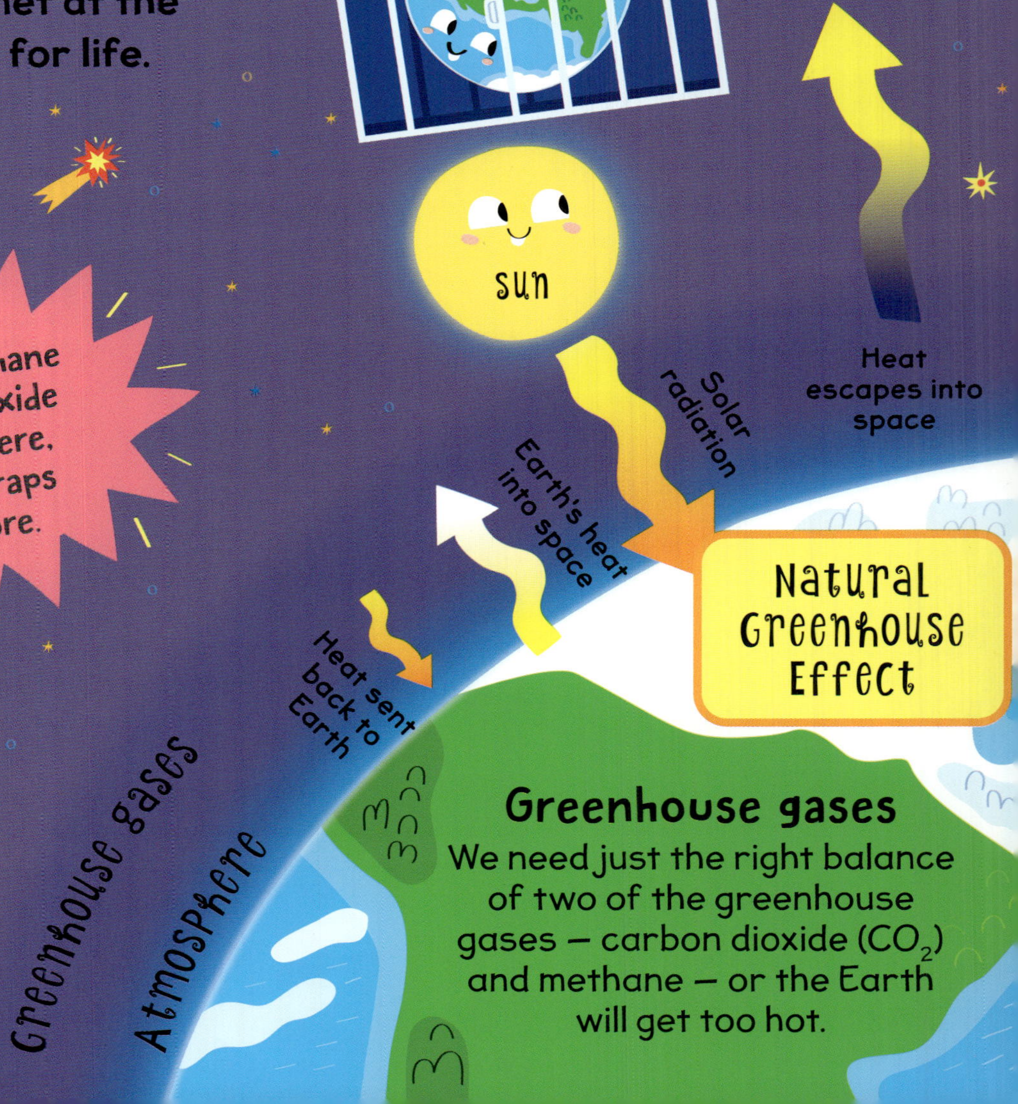

The gases that stop heat escaping into space are called greenhouse gases.

Greenhouse gases

We need just the right balance of two of the greenhouse gases – carbon dioxide (CO_2) and methane – or the Earth will get too hot.

Too hot!

In the last 200 years humans have been burning more fuel than ever, causing Earth's temperature to rise. This is called climate change, and it's affecting the planet's sea levels, ice caps, and weather patterns.

I CAN... USE UP CARBON DIOXIDE

Plants are great because they take in carbon dioxide. Find out what types of tree or plant grow well where you live, and grow a new one from a seed or nut.

A burning problem

When we burn oil, coal, and gas, we release extra greenhouse gases. The gases trap too much heat in the atmosphere, which warms the whole planet. This is called global warming.

Energy everywhere!

Follow this trail to see how the Sun's energy ends up inside you, and what energy we waste along the way.

1 The Sun's energy is in sunlight, which travels through space to Earth.

2 Plants use the energy in sunlight to make food, which they store in their leaves, roots, and seeds.

When plants make food from sunlight they also make oxygen, which we need to breathe!

6 Using a car to go to the shops or a market burns even more energy and creates even more pollution.

7 Cooking the eggs uses energy too, whether it's using gas, oil, or electricity.

3 Chickens eat leaves, roots, and seeds, which give them the energy to live, grow, and lay eggs.

Chickens

Chicken poop can be used to make fertilizer, which helps plants grow.

4 Now the Sun's energy has turned into food – it's inside these eggs!

Eggs

Transport

Cardboard egg boxes, and eggshells can be used to make **compost**.
See page 43.

5 Taking the eggs to market by truck burns fuel, uses up energy, and pollutes the air.

8 Eating the eggs has given this girl energy to play soccer. All living things need energy to move and grow.

I CAN... "SEE" HOW PLANTS TRAP SUNLIGHT

Cut a shape out of aluminium foil and place it over the leaf of a houseplant. Secure it with a paperclip so sunlight can't get through. After a week, remove the foil. What's happened?

Fossil fuels

When we burn oil, gas, and coal for energy, we use fossil fuels, which give off polluting gases. To save our planet, we need to cut down on using them.

Useful energy

We use the energy from fossil fuels to make electricity, to light and heat our homes, and to power machines.

Greenhouse gases are harmful gases given off when we burn wood and fossil fuels

Electricity is a type of energy.

Running out

Oil, gas, and coal are called fossil fuels, because they come from fossils deep underground. This source of energy will run out soon.

Most cars burn gasoline or diesel made from oil to release energy to fuel the engine

Power Plant

Greenhouse gases damage the Earth and pollute our precious **atmosphere**.

Fossils are millions of years old and contain carbon.

Bacteria, plankton, algae, and plants form fossil fuels.

Animals, plants, and fungi get their energy from the Sun or from the food they eat.

I can...save energy

By turning off electric lights when you leave an empty room, you can help save energy that can then be used elsewhere.

Energy from wood

We can get heat and light from burning things too, such as wood. Many people around the world burn wood to heat their homes and to cook.

Going green

We don't need to burn fossil fuels. We can use green energy instead – types of energy that won't run out and don't make greenhouse gases.

Solar power

Solar panels catch the Sun's energy and turn it into electricity. We can put solar panels on buildings or create solar farms.

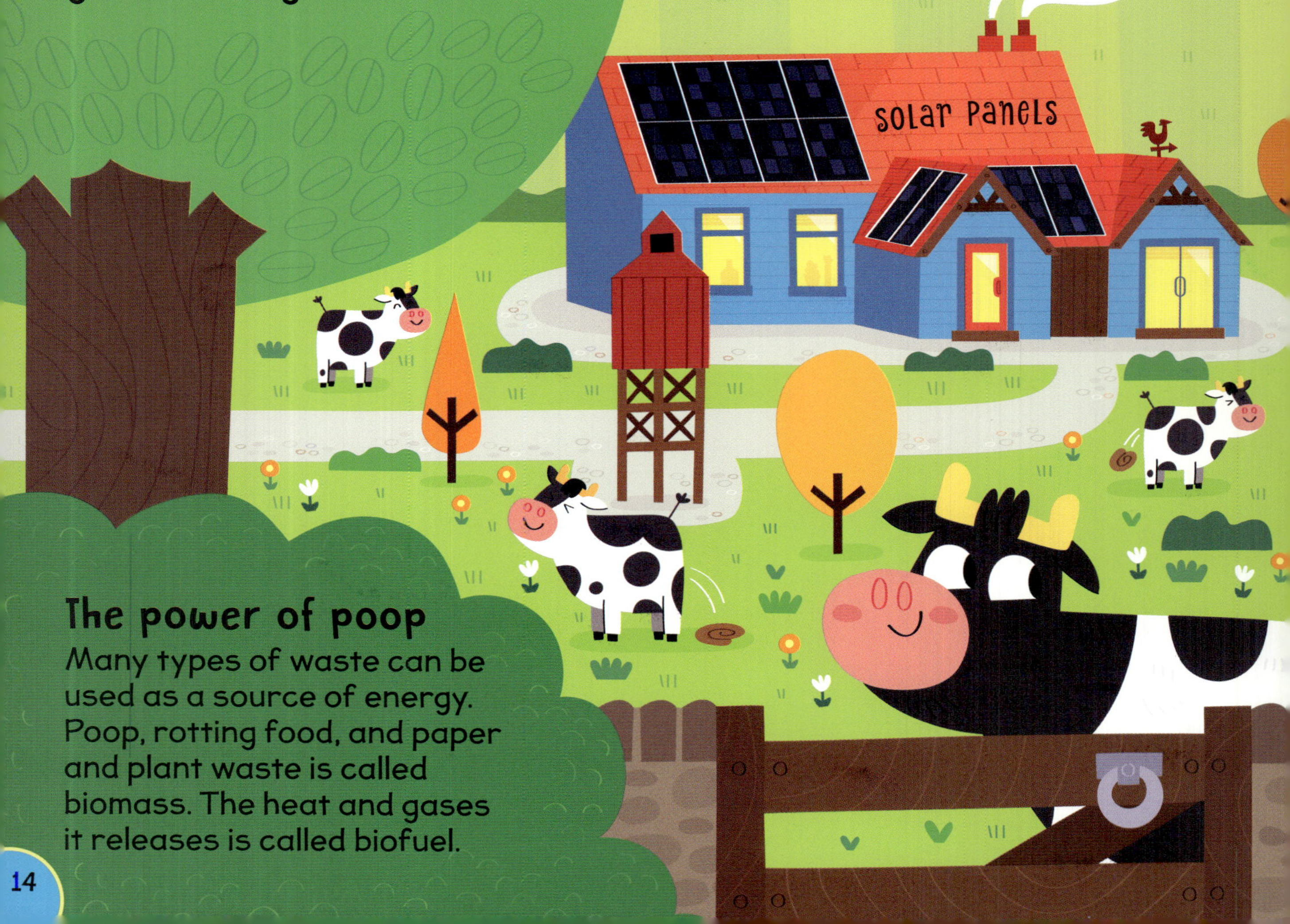

The power of poop

Many types of waste can be used as a source of energy. Poop, rotting food, and paper and plant waste is called biomass. The heat and gases it releases is called biofuel.

Wind power

Wind turbines work best in windy climates. The turbines spin and generate electricity.

Hydropower Plant

Wind turbine

A group of wind turbines is called a wind farm.

About 20 percent (one fifth) of the world's electricity comes from hydropower.

Hydropower

Fast-flowing water is full of energy. The water turns turbines inside a hydropower plant, creating electricity.

I CAN... USE WIND POWER

Make the most of wind's wonderful drying power by helping a grown-up to hang up the wet laundry outside. How many activities or sports can you think of that use wind power?

Cables take the electricity from a hydropower plant to the town.

Sun, wind, and rain

Knowing about the weather allows us to keep an eye on how our climate (the general weather in an area) is gradually changing over time.

Water cycle

As the Sun heats water, it turns into vapor and evaporates into the air. As water vapor condenses, it forms clouds, and water falls as rain. It collects in rivers and flows back into the ocean.

I CAN... MEASURE THE WEATHER

Use a thermometer to keep a temperature diary. Record the temperature at the same time every day, in the same place. How does it change?

The Sun heats the atmosphere and the atmosphere heats the land and water

Measure the weather

Weather scientists are called meteorologists. They calculate how much rain falls and how windy it is, and measure the temperature to find out if places are getting warmer or cooler.

Water wise

More than two-thirds of our planet is covered in water, so why do we have to worry about using too much of it?

A salty problem

Most of the world's water is in the seas and oceans, and is salty. We can't drink it or use it to grow plants.

I CAN... REUSE WATER

Try these ways to reuse fresh water at home:

- Save cooking water and shower water in a bucket and, when it's cool, use it to water plants.
- Collect unused water from water bottles to use for washing up.

Clean it up!

Our fresh water comes from rain, which falls onto the land and flows into lakes and rivers. We collect it and clean it, so it's safe for us to use, but that uses up lots of energy!

Saving water saves energy and that helps to save our planet!

Don't leave taps running! In just one minute, you'll waste the same as 24 glasses of water!

Be smart about water

Think twice before wasting water. Turn off the tap when you brush your teeth. Take showers instead of baths and sponge off stains on your clothes (so you can wear them more times before washing them).

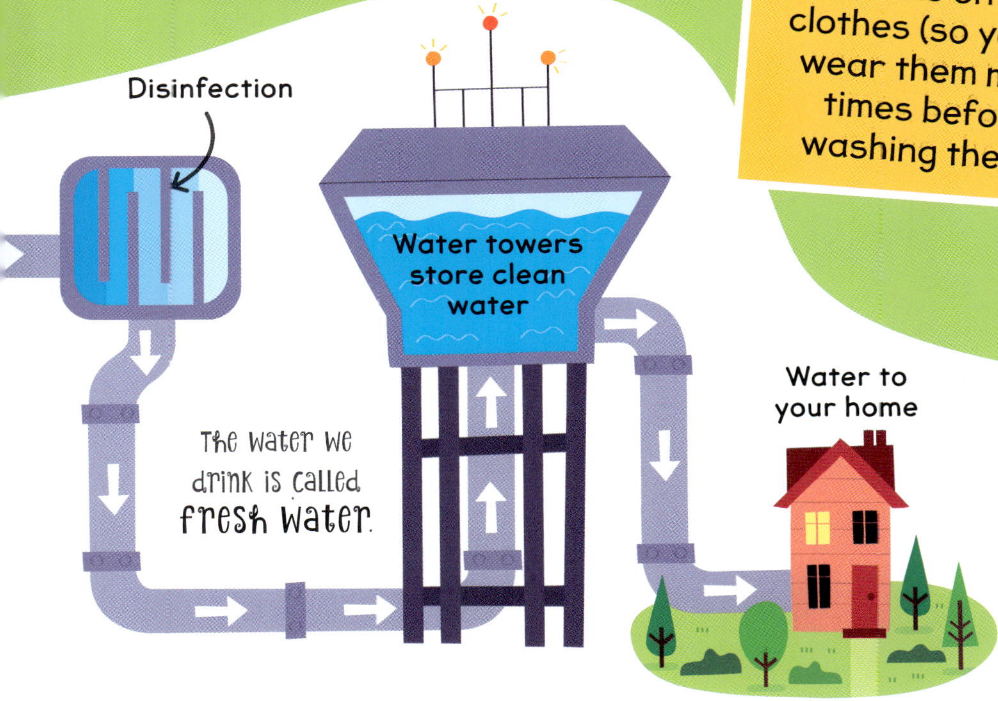

The water we drink is called **fresh water**.

Collect **rainwater** in a rain barrel and use it for watering the garden.

SOS: Save Our Seas

Our incredible oceans are a super-soup of living things, providing us with food, and helping to make and control our weather. But our oceans are in trouble.

Dirty water

Dirty oceans are a growing problem. Trash thrown in rivers often ends up in the ocean. Litter left on the beach gets carried out to sea.

Bye-bye fish

People are eating twice as much fish as they did 50 years ago. So in some places of the world, animals that also eat fish could run out of food.

When you visit the beach, **Leave nothing behind**. Take all of your litter home with you.

I CAN... SAVE FISH

See if you can replace some of your favorite fish dishes with ocean-friendly ingredients. Use the Internet to search recipes for vegan fish sticks.

Litter harms ocean wildlife and pollution is killing coral reefs.

Discarded nets and fishing gear injure and kill ocean creatures.

Happy holidays

Always try to be an ocean-friendly tourist!

- Do not buy souvenirs made from sand, fish, shells, or coral.
- Watch the wildlife, but don't disturb it.
- Travel to beaches by public transport.
- Check that your sunscreen is organic – with no harmful chemicals.

Helping habitats

The place where an animal or plant lives is called its habitat. It's a home! An ocean, a desert, a river, and a rainforest are all types of large habitat.

Little homes

Habitats can also be small. A tree is a habitat for many animals, fungi, and plants. If you look closely, you'll find other habitats inside the tree.

I CAN... HELP BUGS

Make a bug habitat in a garden, park, or woods. Collect old wood, sticks, and leaves and build everything into a pile somewhere cool and shady where it won't be disturbed. Bugs will move into this home-made habitat.

Precious places

Habitats are precious places. Living things find shelter, food, and water there. Sadly, when we dig for fossil fuels or construct roads and buildings, we destroy habitats.

Rewilding

Once a habitat has been damaged, it takes many years to repair it. Restoring an area back to its natural state, with all the animals and plants that belong there, is called rewilding.

Ecosystems

A pond is a type of ecosystem – a collection of living things that all need each other to survive.

An ecologist is a person who studies ecosystems, and works to protect them.

Citizen scientist

The first step to protecting habitats is choosing one to explore. A pond is a habitat for many types of animal.

I CAN... BE A SCIENTIST

Find out about citizen science projects where you live, and join in with a wildlife count.

Citizen scientists also help keep habitats litter-free.

What are citizen scientists?

They are ordinary people who volunteer to help scientists find out about the natural world. Local wildlife groups set up wildlife counts every year.

From farm to plate

We can help the natural world by buying food produced by farmers who try to limit the effects of farming. They take care of the habitats in and around their farms.

Caring farmers

Many farmers try to use green energy. They care about wildlife and try to stop farm waste getting into local rivers.

Organic farming

Organic farms avoid using chemicals to control weeds and pests. They prefer to use natural fertilizers to improve their crops.

Cutting down trees

As the number of humans on the planet grows, farmers need more land to grow more crops to feed us. Huge areas of land, once habitats for wildlife, are cleared.

Deforestation

Rainforests are cleared to make room for cattle, soybean, sugarcane, cocoa, and palm oil trees.

Reforestation

I CAN... SAY NO TO PALM OIL

Palm oil is often used to make chips, cookies, and cakes. Check ingredients to find other products without palm oil, if you can.

Fill it up

Using refillable containers to buy food saves energy. It cuts the amount of packaging and energy that is used to transport food.

Eat green

We can eat wisely to help to save our planet. There are some simple steps we can all take to make sure that our food is green – in a good way!

Check **labels** to find out what food is made of and where it comes from.

Food miles

The distance food travels to get from where it grew to your plate is measured in food miles. The further food travels, the more energy is used.

These freshly-picked oranges travel by truck to get to a boat.

Then they cross the ocean.

They're taken by truck to a supermarket.

Once they're purchased, they might be taken home by car.

This adds up to a lot of miles!

I CAN... TRACK FOOD MILES

Investigate bananas, oranges, and apples to find out where they grow and how far they must travel to reach your home (their food miles).

Grow your own

The most local foods are the ones you grow yourself! You don't need a garden to grow fruit, veggies, or herbs – a window box or balcony is perfect.

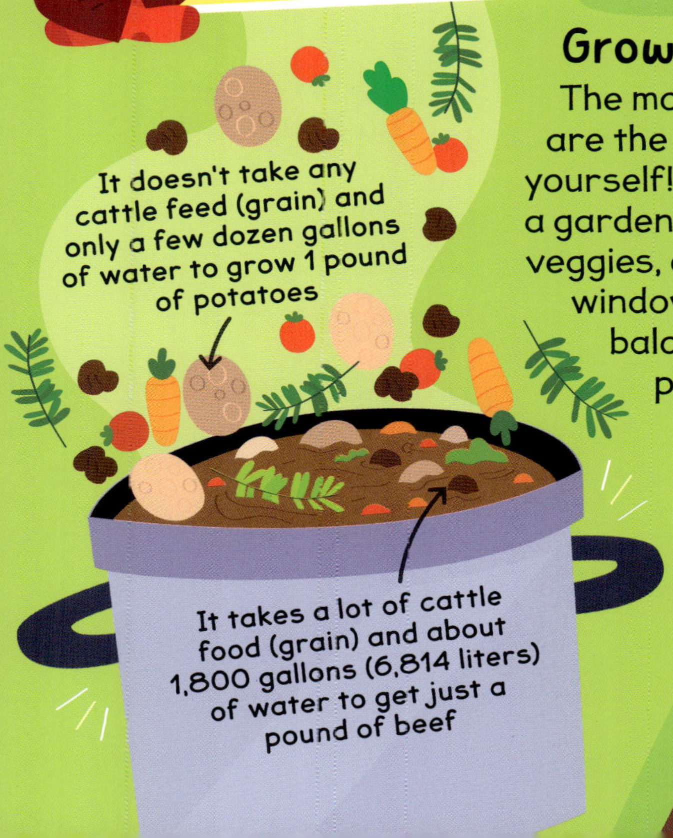

Go veggie

Vegetarians eat a diet without meat and fish. Vegans avoid anything that comes from animals. These diets use less energy and water.

On your bike

Planes, trains, cars, and buses all use energy to move. Most vehicles get their energy by burning gas or diesel, creating deadly pollution.

Traveling by train is three times greener than traveling by car. Trains produce far fewer greenhouse gases.

Brilliant buses

Buses are a great way to transport lots of people, especially if they're electric or run on clean hydrogen!

Electric scooters and bikes are starting to replace cars in cities.

Future flying

Planes are filthy! They burn huge amounts of fossil fuels. New biofuel (made from waste products) could cut the amount of greenhouse gases released by up to 80 percent!

I CAN… WALK AND TALK

Try to walk to your destination whenever possible and play story-tag. One person starts a story and you take turns to continue the tale.

Electric boats make use of waterways to keep city centers free of polluting cars, but electricity still has to come from somewhere.

If we lined up all the world's cars, they would stretch around the world more than 100 times.

People power

Most journeys are often a few miles. Try to walk, bike, or scooter if you can. Using your own energy to travel keeps you fit and healthy too!

Material matters

This book is made from wood that comes from trees. Like glass, plastic, and metal, wood is a material and we use materials to make all sorts of things.

Renewable materials

When a tree is cut down, we can replace it by growing another. We can even mash up old paper and cardboard to turn into new paper.

Natural materials

Many renewable materials come from the natural world. Cotton, wool, wood, stone, leather, clay, and metals are all natural materials.

Metals, such as gold, iron, tin, and aluminium come from rocks.

Glass

Did you know that glass is made from sand? It's mixed with ash and limestone, then melted down in giant ovens. Glass is renewable – it can be crushed into pieces, melted, and turned into new glass.

I CAN... COLLECT MATERIALS

Collecting and reusing old materials is called recycling. Collect magazines, straws, cardboard, and containers to use for craft projects.

Plastic blaster!

One of the world's most useful materials is plastic. It can be made into almost any shape and is strong, long-lasting, cheap to make, and light to carry. So what's the problem with it?

Gone forever

Plastic is made from oil, so when we burn oil to make it, the oil is gone forever. It is a non-renewable resource.

What a rotten material!

Plastic doesn't rot. It lasts for hundreds of years, turning into smaller pieces called microplastics, which animals swallow.

I CAN... DITCH THE PLASTIC!

- Try to buy loose fruit and vegetables, not in plastic packaging.
- Avoid glitter (plastic-coated foil) in crafts.
- Use wooden or metal cutlery, not plastic.
- Take a reusable water bottle out with you.

Scientists are finding new ways to make plastic from things like sugar, straw, corn, and potatoes!

The world produces more than 380 million tons of plastic every year.

Dress smart

Clothes are made from fabrics that can be natural or synthetic (man-made). Choose new clothes carefully and take care of the ones you have.

Wool and cotton

Wool comes from the fleece, or fur, of sheep and other animals. Cotton comes from cotton plants. Both these natural materials can be recycled.

Check labels before you buy clothes. Are they made from renewable or recycled fabrics?

Growing cotton plants takes lots of water and pesticides. It takes about 700 gallons (2,650 liters) of water to make a cotton T-shirt.

Recycled Plastic

Some synthetic fabrics, like nylon and polyester, are made from a type of plastic that can be recycled.

Synthetic fabrics

Many synthetic fabrics are made using nonrenewable materials. If they're burned, they release fumes and can take up to 200 years to break down.

I CAN... GIVE AWAY CLOTHES

Sort out your unwanted clothes to give to charity or friends and family. Ripped or worn clothing can go to a recycling center.

When some synthetic clothes are washed, tiny microfibers of plastic are released.

35 percent of all microplastics going into the ocean come from washing synthetic clothes

What a waste!

Every day, we throw paper, food, plastic, and other precious materials into trash cans. Where does all that trash end up?

Deadly fires

Lots of the world's trash is burned in incinerators, which releases chemicals, gases, and clouds of ash into the air.

Gas from a million tons of landfill waste could power thousands of houses.

Incinerator

I CAN... SORT OUT THE TRASH

Instead of throwing stuff away, try to think if you can do something else with it. Make a poster for school or home to help people work out what can be reused or recycled.

Toxic trash

Most of our trash is taken to landfill sites (huge holes in the ground). Some of it breaks down, leaking chemicals into the soil and methane gas into the air.

Trash to gas

In some parts of the world, methane from landfills is being used as fuel. That helps to cut down the fossil fuels we use, but it would be better if we threw away less.

Time to break down

- Orange peel = 6 months
- Cotton T-shirt = 5 months
- Rubber band = 1 year
- Shoes = 40 years
- Battery = 100 years
- Plastic straw = 200 years
- Aluminium drink can = 80-100 years
- Diaper = 450 years
- Plastic bottle = 500 years
- Plastic bag = 1,000 years

Reduce and reuse

Using a second-hand laptop saves 386 pounds of toxic chemicals!

How can we cut down the amount of energy we use, stop wasting materials, and create less pollution?

Reduce

We can reduce the amount of energy we use if we cut down on the amount of things we buy. Try these simple things – they all save money too!

Reuse

Give your belongings a new life by reusing them, which helps reduce energy and waste. How many of these ideas will you try, for the good of the planet?

1 Use toilet roll tubes to grow seeds. Stack them upright in a container and fill with compost before popping a seed in each one.

2 Use old plastic bottles to play an indoor game of bowling.

I CAN... MAKE A MINIATURE GARDEN

Clean, empty glass jars make great terrariums (bottle gardens). Grow small plants or give them as presents.

3 Set up a swap shop where you can swap clothes, toys, and books with your friends.

4 Cut up old sheets and towels into small squares to use as cleaning cloths.

80 percent of plastic toys end up in landfills or are burned in incinerators.

Recycle now!

The amount of waste we throw away is growing every year. Recycling is one of the easiest ways we can make a difference.

Why recycle?

Many materials, such as glass, plastic, paper, and metals, can be recycled. It cuts the amount of waste going to landfills and incinerators too.

Recycling one tin can save enough energy to power a television for 3 hours.

Recycling one plastic bottle saves enough energy to power a light bulb for 3 hours.

Recycling one glass bottle saves enough energy to power a computer for 25 minutes.

Feed the worms!

Worms are great for recycling. These little wrigglers burrow through soil, munching up bits of vegetation into compost, which helps plants to grow.

1 Glass is collected from recycling bins, taken to a treatment center, washed, and sorted by color.

2 The glass is crushed and melted in giant ovens called furnaces.

A big glass furnace can recycle one million glass bottles and jars every day!

Glass

A glass bottle can take up to a million years to break down! Thankfully, bottles and jars can easily be recycled and turned into new glass.

3 The hot, soft glass is shaped into new bottles and jars, then cooled, ready to be used again.

I CAN... BUILD A COMPOST HEAP

Recycle food waste by creating your own compost heap. Add food scraps, shredded paper, eggshells, and grass cuttings to keep the worms happy.

Things that increase a carbon footprint

Carbon footprints are measured in tons of carbon.

Carbon footprints

Your carbon footprint is how much carbon dioxide (a greenhouse gas) your actions are putting into the air. The smaller your carbon footprint, the better!

I CAN... CUT MY CARBON FOOTPRINT

Set up one jar with a green label and one with a red label. When you do something to reduce your carbon footprint, put a pebble in the green jar. Done something to increase your carbon footprint? Pop a pebble in the red jar! Make sure the green jar is filling faster than the red one.

Things that help to reduce a carbon footprint

Shrink it!

Using energy from fossil fuels adds more to your carbon footprint, but you can shrink it by taking some positive steps.

The future

All over the world, scientists are working hard to find ways to cut the amount of harm we're doing to our beautiful planet.

Green buildings

Trees and plants could cover new buildings. The plants clean the air while keeping buildings warm in winter and cool in summer.

In the future, everything we buy could be marked with its carbon footprint.

Clean the air

Giant vacuum cleaners could be used to suck greenhouse gases out of the air and store them back underground.

Eat bugs!

In some countries, ants, snails, and crickets are considered tasty, healthy treats, and in the future even more of us may be eating bugs!

I CAN... MAKE CHANGES TODAY!

Now that you've read this book, decide on the changes you want to make to your life today. Then lend the book to someone else, so they can read it too.

Do you remember?

The information to answer these questions can be found in this book.

1 What is the blanket of gases wrapped around Earth called?

2 What are fossil fuels?

3 Does burning fossil fuels lower or raise the temperature of Earth?

4 Are there other forms of energy we could use instead?

5 How many types of climate can you remember?

6 How much of our planet is made up of salty water?

7 What is rewilding?

8 What is plastic made from?

9 Where does most of our trash go?

10 What three things beginning with R can you do every day to help our planet?

ANSWERS

1 Atmosphere
2 Coal, oil, and gas
3 Raises the temperature (this is climate change)
4 Yes. Wind power, solar power, hydropower
5 Tropical, desert, temperate, Arctic
6 97 percent
7 Restoring a habitat (where an animal or plant lives) back to its natural state
8 Oil (it is a nonrenewable material)
9 To landfill sites or incinerators
10 Reduce, reuse, recycle